Demonstrate It!

Unleashing Healing, Signs, and Wonders

Troy Anthony Smith

©Copyright 2011 by Troy Anthony Smith. All rights reserved. No part of this publication may be reproduced, distributed, or transmitted in any form or by any means, including photocopying, recording, or other electronic or mechanical methods, without the prior written permission of the publisher, except in the case of brief quotations embodied in critical reviews and certain other noncommercial uses permitted by copyright law. For permission requests, write to the publisher, addressed "Attention: Permissions Coordinator," at the address below.

Dunimus Media,LLC
600 S. Spring Street
Los Angeles,CA 90014
www.dunimus.com

www.demonstrateit.org

Ordering Information:
Quantity sales. Special discounts are available on quantity purchases by corporations, associations, and others. For details, contact the publisher at the address above.

Orders by U.S. trade bookstores and wholesalers. Please contact Dunimus Media: Tel: (888) 949-4334 or visit www.dunimus.com.

Printed in the United States of America

ISBN- 978-0-9849953-1-8

I wrote this book simply because it needed to be written. I didn't seek out to become a best selling author or have a global ministry. I'm just a guy who read the Bible and became outraged at the the stark contrast between what Jesus and the early apostles accomplished and what the church of present day is doing. Since discovering who I am in Christ, I have four simple truths which this entire book is based upon:

1. Jesus Christ is the Son of God, the Word of God, and cannot fail. He is the same yesterday, today and forever

2. Everywhere He went He totally destroyed the effects of the devil

3. Through faith in Jesus, we have become born again sons of the Most High God and made joint heirs with Christ

4. Now everywhere we go we totally destroy the effects of the devil

As you read through the teachings in this book I want these four truths to resonate within you and cause you to act. You have been given authority over all the works of the devil, such as sin, poverty, depression, sickness, and disease. The entire world is waiting on you to be who Jesus died for you to become.

Contents

Intro 11

A Little About Me 15

1. Would The Real Church Please Stand UP 25

2. Would The Real Church Please Stand UP (Part 2) 29

3. Make a Decision to Be A Miracle Worker! 33

4. Knowing Who You Are 37

5. Knowing Who You Are (Part 2) 43

6. Who Truly is Called? 47

7. Hearing from God- Was that from Me, God, or the Devil? 51

8. The Prophetic vs. The Psychic 55

9. The Secret Key to Prophesying Accurately 59

10. The Nutritional Value of the Word 65

11. Let's Talk About Faith 69

12. Faith vs Belief 73

13. Hope: The Starting point of Faith 77

14. Simplifying the Gifts of the Spirit 81

15. Can Everyone Be Healed? 85

16. Focus On the Mission, and Stop trying to Predict His Return 89

17. The Authority to Heal 93

18. Because of Your Unbelief…...97

19. Activating the Laws of Healing..101

20. Which Kingdom do You Serve? 105

21. Prosperity Gone Wrong 111

Conclusion 117

Intro

The sad truth is that most Christians do not understand truly what the Gospel is. Over the years, the meaning has been lost in bad translations, CNN and History Channel specials, TBN sound bites, dead church services, and political debates. How can the church truly be powerful, if we don't even know what the Gospel is? So before we can discuss divine healing, or prophetic utterances, or anything, we must have this clear understanding on what the gospel is, and what it is not.

So what is the Gospel? Is it just a style of music, like Hip Hop or Country, as in *Gospel Music*? Or is it that Jesus died on the cross? Is it that we get to go to heaven when we die?

The word Gospel, just by itself means 'Good News'. So the word just by itself could describe any kind of good news. The Gospel of the Philadelphia Eagles, is the good news of them winning the Super Bowl (if you're an Eagle fan like me). But the specific Gospel that Jesus spoke about was the Gospel of the Kingdom (of God). All throughout the scriptures, Jesus walked around declaring and demonstrating the Kingdom of God or the Kingdom of Heaven. Simply put, the Kingdom of God, is God's way of doing things, or his system of operating. The kingdom of heaven is the same thing, because God is in heaven. So anywhere in the Bible where Jesus is explaining the kingdom of God, he is simply talking about God's way of doing things. If we were talking about the Kingdom of Mike Brown, we would be talking about Mike Brown's, way of doing things.

So what is this kingdom of God, what is God's way of doing things? Jesus instructed in Matthew 6:33 to seek the kingdom of God, and all things (possessions, food, clothing, etc) would be added to us. In another passage , Jesus describes the Kingdom of God as a rich treasure found in a field. When a man discovered this treasure, he sold all his possessions in order to purchase that field. (Matthew 13:44). To understand the Kingdom of God, you must first understand that the way things are happening now on the Earth are twisted (in God's eyes). Due to Adam's fall in Genesis, we live in a fallen, backwards society (known as the world's system). In the world's system the following things are commonplace: Depression, sickness, disease, lack, greed, lust, hopelessness, and more. All of these horrible things were going on in Jesus' days, just as they are going on today. However, Jesus steps onto the scene and establishes a new way (God's way). The people were all astonished. Jesus addresses the crowd (in my own words), *'I know all you guys have been struggling here, but look, the way we do it in heaven, that's how we are about to do it down here. Is anybody sick? It's time for your healing, because there is no sickness in heaven. Is anyone broke? I'm going to show you how to prosper. Are there any broken hearts out there? That too can be fixed. Look everybody, I know things have been messed up for awhile here, but I came to take care of all of that, I came to set you guys free, if you want to be.' (Luke 4:18)*

Contrary to popular opinion, Jesus did not walk around talking about himself. His sole message was the Kingdom of God; the message was that anything that does not line up with how heaven operates, should not occur down here one earth. The result? Blind eyes were opened, the lame men were walking, demons were cast out of people, and debts were cancelled, all because the Kingdom of God invaded the earth. Not only did he declare this kingdom of God, everywhere he went, but he demonstrated it. Then he goes and tells 70 of his followers to declare and demonstrate the same thing. The 70 had the same exact results Jesus had. He later told his followers that this Gospel of the Kingdom should be preached in all nations, and then the end shall come.(Matthew 24:14).

Is this being preached today? Not likely. Most churches today do not even believe God still heals people. Jesus had one message, and expected us to continue to carry it out. Most of the messages we hear today are a lot of motivational clichés, and at the end an altar call saying that Jesus died for your sins, and if you want to go to heaven when you die, come to the altar. Yes, Jesus did die and rose again, and yes you definitely must believe that, however that is not the full Gospel of the Kingdom. That is just the starting point. Jesus was crucified and rose from the dead, and his blood paid the price for our sins, so that we would have a right to be free in all areas, in this life, and after we die.

The Gospel of the Kingdom is not a 'when we die' message. It is a right now message. The message is that through Jesus, whatever you are struggling with, can be made right. Any crooked path can be made straight. Whether it is sickness, your marriage, your money, your children, anything. Jesus' name literally means 'Deliverer' and that is exactly what he came to do, deliver you from any bad situation. Jesus Christ, the same yesterday, today, and forever. If you believe that the gospel of the Kingdom is a message about having the right to go to heaven when you die, you totally missed it. The gospel of the kingdom is about the right for heaven to get into you!

Now that is the message that should be preached from every streetcorner.

A Little About Me

I can recall as a young boy, I would read the Bible and be totally amazed by it. Specifically the book of Acts. It was as if I could sense the excitement among the people of that day as the miracles were exploding on the scene. As I would read it, I would imagine what it would be like if those same 'acts' took place today. My body would be filled with sheer excitement as I would envision laying hands on the blind and sick people and watching them get healed, just as Jesus and the apostles did it. 'Wouldn't that be awesome!' I thought in my mind.

Then my world came crashing down as I was told from the Pastor of the church that my family attended that those things no longer happen. I was told that healings and miracles all passed away and stopped after the early apostles died. Suddenly church became very boring to me. I was surrounded by individuals who had no more of a relationship with Jesus, than I had with my elementary school principle. Yes, we knew the principal's name and where the principal's office was located, but we never spoke to her, and the only time we thought she wanted to speak to us is when we were in trouble. Doesn't that sound like the relationship most Christians today have with Jesus?

After being shut down by that Pastor when I was about 12 years old, I spent years out of God's presence. In my thinking, why serve a God who is totally absent from the lives of His people? Even though I was fascinated by the stories of Joshua stopping the sun, Elijah calling down fire, and Paul performing miracles, I was led to believe those were basically folklore or similar to Greek mythology. I went on to college and later pursued a career in the music industry and never really thought much about God after my early years.

Then one night I came home from being out at the club partying, (quite intoxicated) and I flipped on the TV to see what was on. A lady was on preaching, but there was something different about her words. It was as if she was speaking *directly* to me. She told me that I had just came home from the club, and that I was wandering, but that God had a plan for my life and that He was going to use me to do a mighty work. Now this totally creeped me out and I instantly sobered up and tried to change the channel. But my arm froze up on me and I couldn't move to get the remote.

The next day I received a thought in my head to go see a guy who used to be a rapper who is now a Pastor in Atlanta. I googled his name to find out where he was in Atlanta and found out his church was right across the street from my condo. I went to his church that Sunday and the strangest thing happened. In the middle of his sermon, he turns to me (I had never met him before) and he begins to prophesy and says the same exact thing that the lady told me the previous night. I was totally wacked out after all of this because I was told that things like that no longer occurred.

Shortly after that experience I totally gave my life over to God and was filled with the Holy Spirit. I then spent about

6 months where I basically didn't leave my condo, just read the Word and prayed all day and listened to sermons. My friends and family thought I had lost my mind! I didn't lose it, I was discovering it. When I resurfaced I had 2 questions that I had to answer. 1), why would anyone purposely convince others that healing, signs and wonders had ceased 2) those that know about signs and wonders, why does it seem like they keep it to themselves?

Those questions have been the focus of the launch of the ministry Demonstrate It. We have been charged with demonstrating this glorious gospel, not in the back alleyways and hidden places but in the most visible areas of society. After being a marketing professional in the entertainment industry for many years, the one thing I totally understood was that if you have an amazing product, you want to display it on every billboard, bus, and magazine. We have a product that is more dynamic than anything that this world has ever seen, yet you have to do an intense Google search just to find out about divine healing or prophecy.

We might be just starting, but I don't believe in keeping this thing a secret...

I share my personal testimony so that others may begin to live the life that we were destined to live. I'm not trying to impress anyone, but simply impress upon you the power that is lying dormant within you. Sometimes when we read the gospels, we look at the mighty acts of Jesus and say wow, but that is Jesus, I could never do that. Yet he said 'the work I do, you shall do even greater'. In John 17, when He was about to back to the Father, he even said, 'The glory that you have given Me (he was speaking to the Father) I have given them (referring to you and me). So my question to everyone reading this is, what have you done with the glory that God the Father has given you?

After being filled with the Holy Spirit in the Fall of 2004, I was totally amazed by his power and precious love. Amazed is definitely an understatement, there are no words that can describe what I was going through at that time. Growing up in NJ and even going to college in Florida, I had never imagined that tongues, prophecy, miracles, and healing were still in existence. My mind went back to my youth reading those stories in the book of Acts and rekindling that excitement. Days became weeks, and weeks became months as I would spend every waking moment in the presence of the Holy Spirit. I would study his Word for hours upon hours, getting more excited with each passing day. I am fully convinced that this whole thing was ordained by the Holy Spirit, as the church I was going to began to have daily services for about 2 months on the subject of mind renewal.

For the next six years I served faithfully at that church, absorbing every message, instruction, and opportunity. We held daily morning prayer services at 6am, which I used to lead many mornings. This was when I first came into contact with the power of God. While leading the people into worship, I would notice a shift in the atmosphere, almost like a purity beyond explanation. Many times during this worship I would see people in the congregation being set free from demonic oppression. We also delivered many after the prayer service and the congregation went home. Later I served over the prayer room, the place where people go after they come to the altar to receive salvation, be filled with Holy Spirit, or deliverance from oppression. I didn't necessarily receive any training on how to pray for the sick, I would just watch my Pastor lay hands on them and they would be healed based upon the Word. So I did the same thing. After every service in the back prayer room, there were scores of men and woman either needing to be healed or an encouraging Word from God; so by faith I just went for it. The results were nothing short of miraculous. I would see them healed right in front of me! Testimonies would come back about the prophetic words that I had spoken during these sessions and how it impacted their lives.

After seeing the results I was getting inside the church I began to wonder how far this thing could go. *Could it work outside the four walls of the church?* I began to lay hands on people that I would see with ailments at the grocery store, on the street corners, anywhere and everywhere. I learned the power of God works everywhere, just have faith and let it rip! It was truly amazing.

I noticed that if I was bold enough to step out on faith, God would always show up. He never let me down. If I would open my mouth, He would give me a prophetic utterance. But if I was too afraid to approach someone, then nothing would happen. Many are stuck in this phase because they are too afraid to approach people. This is where love comes in. The gifts of the Spirit are all activated by love, but the opposite of love is selfishness. *'What are people going to say if they don't get healed? How am I going to look if my prophetic word is way off? What if it doesn't work?'* All these doubts are all selfish based and will cause a person to never ever step out. The most important thing to remember when ministering, is that it is not about *you*, it's all about helping *them*.

I was on a quest to learn all that I could about the healing power of God. I began to study the healing evangelists of the 20s, 30s, and 40s, and the two that resonated deep within me were John G. Lake and Smith Wigglesworth. I was especially drawn to John G. Lake because the people who he discipled had the same results that he had, if not greater. His teaching on healing goes against what most ministries teach today, yet his results were far greater. A key difference is that today we focus a lot on the anointing of the minister and the minster's gift, but Lake's teaching focused more on our authority in Christ. Every believer can do what Jesus did, because you have been given what Jesus was given. Pretty simple stuff, yet powerful.

So just when I was beginning to get comfortable, God directs me to relocate to Los Angeles, a place I had only been one time before. I didn't really know anybody there, so no Pastors were calling me to preach at their church, and there were no invitations to speak at any revivals or crusades. Yet all of this was a blessing in disguise. This forced me to go out into the highways and street corners to demonstrate the gospel. I moved to Hollywood, where I was a fixture on Hollywood Boulevard laying hands on people and giving prophetic words.

To increase my reach I launched a website that later transformed into a ministry called Demonstrateit.org. The goal was simply to reach people all over the world with the info that I wish I had as a young boy. The info that Jesus is moving in present day with healing power, signs, and miracles, and the power of the Holy Spirit is available to us all. Each night I would be on my computer giving prophetic words to the masses of people who found my site, or going door to door in the poorest neighborhoods praying for sick, lost, or downtrodden. Since our inception, we have received much support, as people from all areas of the country have been inspired to 'demonstrate it', not just talk about it.

So how about you, have you been moved to demonstrate it?

The following are 21 teachings which the Holy Spirit gave me during a one year period in my first year of ministry in Los Angeles. While ministering to the lost, I would come home and chronicle my experiences and share teaching moments with anyone who would listen or read my blog. As a result, I gained quite a following and decided to compile the teachings into this book. There are no particular order to the teachings, just whatever I sensed the Holy Spirit wanted me to say at that particular moment.

1. Would The Real Church Please Stand UP

In many ways the modern day church of today is completely backwards. To fully understand the role of the church, we must fully understand how it was intended to function. But even before you can understand this, you must fully understand and have a clear picture of who Jesus is and what he did during his ministry on the earth. According to 1 John 3:8, the reason Jesus came to the earth was to destroy the works of the devil. He spent his entire 3 and 1/2 year earthly ministry doing this, destroying the works of the devil: healing sickness, lack, demonic oppression, and more. Then He ascended into heaven and left us in charge. The church is the 'body' of Christ, and Jesus is the 'head'. For any task to be carried out, it must be carried out by the body, not the head. Jesus and his body (the church) are one, just like you (your head and your body) are one. Notice in Acts when Paul was persecuting the church, Jesus did not say, 'Why are you persecuting my church?', he said, 'Why are you persecuting *me*'. Jesus was crucified at least 5 years prior to these persecutions, yet he makes no distinction between his church and himself.

Fast forward 2000 years, from Jesus earthly ministry and the first apostles, to present day. The modern church of today very little resembles Jesus. Jesus demonstrated the kingdom of God, and moved in great signs and miracles. What does today's church do? In most churches, people come together once a week on Sunday to be entertained by a choir and good motivational message from the public speaker. Majority of the congregation is sick, in debt, depressed, overweight, living in fornication, and homosexual. The church has become a social club, a meeting place in which you never really have to do anything, just come back next Sunday and give your tithes and offerings. Keep the machine going.

Did Jesus change? Did the mission statement for the 'body of Christ' turn into a non-profit organization like the Red Cross or United Way? Did not Jesus say, 'he that believes in Me the works that I do, shall he do also, and greater works shall he do, because I go to be with the Father?'

The church (the local church) should actually be more of a training center. Believers should come together to hear and be taught the Word of God, and then go out into the streets to affect society. Most of the country now is upset about the direction our nation is heading. Healthcare costs are too high, the debt crisis is spiraling out of control, education system is crumbling, etc. All this is happening because the church has refused to take its rightful place in society. The church literally means in the Greek, 'ekklasia' which comes from two words "ek"- out of, and "kaleo"- shall be called. In the original context in Hellenistic culture it refers to a certain set of people within the Greek city states, who were called out from the general population for the purpose of leading or to take care of special circumstances.

In that same vein, when you received Jesus as Lord and Savior, you were called out from among the general population in whatever country you were from, for the sole purpose of ruling and reigning with Christ to destroy the works of the devil. Once you received Christ you are no longer a Mason, or a Republican, or African American, or Jew, or Democrat, your allegiance first and foremost should be to Jesus as the Body of Christ. So now that Jesus is your head, your official political policy should be to line up with the Word of God. Healthcare? Go lay hands on the sick. Programs for the poor? Teach them God's system of wealth. Debt crises? Owe no man nothing but to love him. Because there is no recession or depression in heaven, we as ambassadors should not stand for it here on earth. Until we as the body of Christ make a stand, things are going to just get worse and worse. God has anointed us to fix all these problems. According to Romans 8:19, all of creation is waiting on the Sons of God to be made manifest in the Earth, to become known.

Would the real church please stop hiding and reveal yourself? Earth is waiting.

2. Would The Real Church Please Stand UP (Part 2)

As Christians we must demonstrate what we believe and not just talk about it. The church must take its rightful place in society, and not be transformed into a mere social club which meets once a week to be entertained. But let's see what God has to say about this. Is God pleased with the modern day church? A passage in Amos, is prophetic utterance by God, describing his thoughts about the church of 2012:

"I can't stand your religious meetings. I'm fed up with your conferences and conventions. I want nothing to do with your religion projects, your pretentious slogans and goals. I'm sick of your fund-raising schemes, your public relations and image-making. I've had all I can take of your noisy ego-music. When was the last time you sang to me? Do you know what I want? I want justice-oceans of it. I want fairness-rivers of it. That's what I want. That's all I want."

-Amos 5:21-24 (Message Translation)

The church should be the most powerful organization in the history of the planet. If we could come together and agree on the basic principles of what Jesus taught, within a matter of days things would change. Stop looking to the government to fix what God called us to fix. In John 17, Jesus prayed that the church would be one, just as He and the Father are one. It is now time to fulfill that passage of scripture.

In 2011 the church, has given enough through tithes and offerings to bail out the US government. There is enough healing power in our hands to not need healthcare. We are the answer to the poor and sick.

Imagine if a wealthy business owner came by your door one day and handed you the cure to AIDS/HIV. In return you agreed to quit your job and move to Africa to distribute this cure. You also agreed to start a new division within the company and hire 10,000 employees to distribute this cure to the ones who needed it the most. Five years go by and the business owner comes back to your door. He finds you sitting on the couch eating pizza with the cure sitting in the refrigerator untouched. How pleased do you think the business owner would be?

That is exactly how heaven views the church of today. We have been given the cure to solve all of the world's problems, yet we are doing nothing with it. In fact, most of the church is so involved in the world's system of solving their problems they refuse to even see what the Word of God declares.

The church is to be a mighty force, backed by the Word of God and the power of the Holy Spirit. Its people cannot fail and its acts shall baffle the world, just as it did in the book of Acts when the Gentiles said, 'The people who have turned the world upside down have come here!' That's right we have come to your city and your country, so brace yourself. We must make a stand for truth, for righteousness.

I am willing to make a stand, are you with me?

3.Make a Decision to Be A Miracle Worker!

I wanted to take some time out today to encourage people to go forth to do the works of Jesus. We launched Demonstrate It not too long ago and the response has been nothing short of overwhelming. However, many people I am finding out just need to be encouraged. Our ministry is not so much about healing as it's about revealing the believer's authority. It is simply telling everyone wherever we go, that the Bible in fact means what is says.

I think over the years instead of just receiving what the Word says, we try to rationalize certain scriptures that our minds simply cannot grasp. For example, in Mark 16, Jesus clearly showed the signs of those that believe: they would cast out devils, speak with new tongues and lay hands on the sick, and they would recover (I'm paraphrasing). Yet some church pastors might say, 'Yeah, it's in the Word, but he wasn't speaking to all Christians, just his early followers.

Another scripture in James, says the prayer of faith shall save the sick. Yet someone will pop up and say, *well maybe it is not his will to heal this person*. If it is in the Word of God, then it *is* the will of God. However, most churches today, will go against these scriptures and justify it by saying a particular scripture was for these people, or this scripture was for this time, and so on. Perfect theology is to look at the life of Jesus. What did he do? Did he **ever** let a person stay in their sickness, or refuse to heal someone?

According to Jesus in Mark 7, traditions make the Word of God of no effect. Traditions are teachings and doctrines that have been passed down over the generations that are not Bible-based, yet people believe them as such. These are also known as sacred cows. In India, where there are millions of starving children, there are hundreds of healthy cows available, but the people will not eat them because they are considered 'sacred'. It is because of these sacred cows in the gospel, that many are starving spiritually today. An example of a sacred cow is the belief that healings, miracles, tongues, and prophecies have passed away.

Another sacred cow is that God no longer speaks today. Many people truly believe this, however, there is a deep desire in a person's innermost being that wants to hear directly from God. Both saved and unsaved people want to know the divine will and purpose for their lives. Should I take this job? Should I marry this guy? A person that truly wants to hear from God, yet believes he no longer speaks today will find themselves at some demonic psychic trying to find out the future. Or seeing some witchdoctor to heal them when the medicine is not working. Or morally degrading or compromising their beliefs for some extra money to pay bills.

Everything in the kingdom of God is based upon belief. Without belief, we have nothing, no experience of any kind. However, this is the exact opposite of the how world thinks. They say things like, 'When I see it, I'll believe it'. Even in science, the premise is to see it, experience it, and test it (and test it again), then we'll believe it. In the kingdom you must believe it first, then you can see it and experience it. If you don't believe it first, and act upon what you believe, you will **never** experience it ever.

Here are some words of wisdom for those who have a hard time believing a particular promise in the Bible. Act like you believe it is so (even before you see it), and then it will happen because you acted upon it. Don't wait on some 'feeling' or even a 'Word' from heaven (you have his Word in the Bible), just go for it. When I decided that I was going to lay hands on the sick and see them healed it was just a decision in my mind. I had never done it before. I had just seen my Pastor do it, I had seen ministers on television do it, and I had even read about evangelists in the 30s, 40s, and 50s do it. But all of this meant nothing until I made up my mind to do it myself.

A few years ago we were having a service at Fort Valley, GA. Several hours before the service, while I was on a college campus, I came across a man on campus walking on crutches.

Now I didn't feel anything. I didn't hear the Holy Spirit tell me to go pray for him. I didn't see 3 angels circling around him with harps and gold dust. I just knew what the Word says concerning healing, and this man needed healing. My mind was telling me I would look like a fool in front of everybody on this campus. Yet the Word instructed me what to do. I asked him if he wanted to be healed today, because it said in the Bible that healing will come if I lay hands on him. (He had severe pain in his foot, and could not put weight on it). He looked at me like I was crazy, but he allowed me pray for him. Now also keep in mind I didn't pray a long 5 minute traditional church prayer such as 'Oh Lord, the great and powerful mighty One of Israel, if it be in thy will to heal this young man...' No, my prayer was about 10 seconds long. Actually it wasn't even a prayer, I spoke directly to his foot, just as Jesus spoke directly to the fig tree. I layed hands on it and commanded his foot to be healed right now in Jesus name. Then I asked him to move it around to see if there was any pain there. He had a look of surprise on his face and said the pain had gone down a lot and he was very thankful. Truthfully I was probably more surprised than he was. Not that I didn't believe in the healing power of God, but actually seeing it in action is a totally different ball game. So I told him I would pray for him again, because we wanted his foot 100% pain free. After the second time he was pain free and no longer needed the crutches.

Also, after the healing he was more open to hear about the gospel, considering Jesus had just visited him personally. For those of you who minister, it is one thing to preach about how Jesus walked around healing the sick in Capernaum and Galilee 2,000 years ago. It is a whole different story to actually demonstrate Jesus healing people in 2012 in Times Square in New York City. That day before we even had service, the power of God showed up everywhere we went, we were laying hands all over campus, prophesying to people, and leading many to Christ.

I truly believe that in this day, the greatest move of God is going to be in the United States. And what is going to make this revival different from the ones in the 30's, 40, and 60s is that it is not going to take place in the church. It is going to take place in the sporting arenas, grocery stores, bars, and streetcorners. Make a decision today that God is going use you for this great revival. It is now time for you to get plugged in!

4. Knowing Who You Are

Do you know who you are today? Many of the problems that believers have today arise because they do not have a clue to their true identity. They pray for things they have already been given, and beg God for things that already belong to them. As a new believer, I would read the Bible and be astonished at the stark contrast between what the Word says, and the lives of the actual people who claimed to be living by it.

Remember the movie the Bourne Identity, starring Matt Damon? In the movie, he plays an assassin who has his memory totally wiped out. As the movie progresses he discovers he has these abilities innate within him to basically be a one man army. It's the same way in the spirit. Once we were born-again and filled with the Holy Spirit, innate within us is the DNA of Jesus Christ. We have the ability to do everything that he did. In fact, he even claimed that we would do greater works than He did. (John 14:12) Now that sounds blasphemous to someone who does not know their place in Christ, yet that is exactly who we are. It's not so much about becoming something or increasing our ability, but just discovering who we are and what we have been created to do.

What? You mean I can walk around just like Jesus did? That's right, in fact that's what He intended. But in order for this to become a reality for you, you must settle 2 things in your heart. The first thing you must settle is that you are complete in Him. You do not need anything else, no other aid or support. The second thing is that the work has already been finished.

Let's settle the fact that you are complete in Him. Most Christians generally do not have a problem believing that when Jesus walked the earth, that He had the fullness of the Godhead in Him. According to Colossians 2:9 (Amplified version) , 'for in Jesus the whole fullness of Deity (the Godhead) continues to dwell in bodily form.' Yet most Christians stop there. The very next verse it states that you too are filled with the Godhead. 'And you are in Him made full and having come to fullness of life [in Christ you too are filled with the Godhead—Father, Son, and Holy Spirit—and reach full spiritual stature].' So in another words, if you are in Christ you are not missing anything. It's like you are a soldier equipped with all the same exact weapons that Jesus was equipped with.

There is a popular teaching going around in some Christian circles that you must receive a 'special' anointing or 'gifting' to do certain things. For example you must receive a 'healing anointing' to pray for the sick or a 'prosperity mantel' or a 'deliverance anointing' to cast out demons. Some believers even go from conference to conference all across the country to pick up anointings and mantels like they are trophies of some kind. All of that is unbiblical, and suggest that somehow you are insufficient as a believer and need to receive 'more'. The only thing you need is the Holy Spirit, all these benefits are included in your born again welcoming package. I suggest you read your new hire material.

Again, you are totally complete in Him. If you are ministering to someone in the street or in school, the reality that you have everything you need to set the person free must overrule any feeling of lack. Inside of you is the ability to cast out any demon, lay hands to heal if you have to, or even prophesy, give a word of encouragement. Allow yourself to be led by the Holy Spirit, remember you are fully equipped to handle the situation. I used to sit in the back of the church and watch the leader lay hands on the sick and watch people get healed. I would think to myself, *'wow, that is amazing, what an awesome gift he has. Too bad I don't have that gift.'* Many Christians feel the same way, that they don't have a particular 'gift' and then never venture out and do the miraculous. To sharpen your abilities it will take time and practice, but settle it once and forever that **you are complete in him**, lacking no ability, gift, or anointing. According to 2 Corinthians 1:21, God has already anointed you.

The second thing you must settle in your heart is that the work of Christ is finished. When Jesus said, 'It is finished' he really did mean it. Most Christians spend days, weeks or even years in condemnation after they make a mistake. Jesus' blood paid all the costs for sin, and God has blotted it out from His memory. According to Romans 8:1, there is **no** condemnation to those that are in Christ Jesus. Why is this important to know? This is important because if you are doing God's work and you make a mistake somewhere, such as a sexual mistake or a financial mistake, you must know that Jesus paid the price for any and all sin; so now repent and move on like it never happened.

This goes against **everything** the world teaches us. They teach you to be in remorse for 10 years, resign from whatever position you had, and basically quit life. Even the church world can be the most condemning, but if you understand that you have been made righteous and nothing can change your right standing with God, just repent and finish your course. Know that God is not holding your sin against you. Paul was heavily criticized for this teaching, as many people thought that this would encourage sin. 'Shall we continue in sin, so that grace may abound. God forbid. How shall we that are dead to sin, live any longer therein' (Rom 6:1). In fact, this highly discourages sin, because once you realize all that He has done for you, sin is the last thing on your mind. Condemnation is one of the enemy's biggest weapons, designed to stop believers from continuing their ministry and be all that God created them to be. When God sees you, all He sees is the blood, and to Him you look like a duplicate of Jesus, without any sin or blemish. Why then would you see yourself any different?

The work is finished concerning your healing. Jesus' shed blood also took care of any and all healing. We now have a divine right to be healed. However with healing, you must activate your spiritual right. An analogy is a class action lawsuit. Imagine that a faulty prescription drug infected millions of individuals, and a lawsuit was filed against this drug. Anyone who took this drug would then be entitled to $1 million dollars. Now even if you took the drug, there still is some action that you must take in order for you to reap the $1 million, as indicated in the class action lawsuit, even though anyone and everyone who took the drug is entitled to the reward. In the same way, everyone is entitled to divine healing, based upon what Jesus did 2,000 years ago, yet we must activate our right to healing, based upon the legally binding paperwork of the Word of God. We activate healing by believing the Word and then releasing your faith; or else the enemy will run all over you and your family with sickness, poverty, depression, and more.

The bottom line is that we are not trying to get God to do something. We don't pray that God would heal Aunt Betty. We don't pray that God will forgive any sin that we might have just committed. What we do is align our thinking with the fact that through Jesus' blood already paid the cost for healing and that through faith we activate it. I thank God that He has already forgiven me of my sin and then repent and move on. It's all about living under grace. Grace is goodness that none of us deserved. Let grace be a reality to you today. Begin to walk in your divine dominion as a son or daughter of the Most High God!

5. Knowing Who You Are (Part 2)

It is vitally important that you know who you are. Do you know why the enemy satan hates you so much? It is because you were created to be what he attempted to be. Lets explore this.

Long before man was created, satan was the archangel Lucifer. He was a beautiful creature, in fact in Ezekiel 28 says he was created perfect, with every precious stone (diamond, onyx, jasper, sapphire, etc) being his covering and his sockets and engravings were gold. He was the anointed cherub who literally walked up and down the stones of fire (in the presence of God). It says he was blameless in all his ways from the day he was created, until iniquity was found in him. It sounds like Lucifer had a nice gig in heaven, so I really wanted to know how everything went so sour. What really happened?

Isaiah 14 sheds more light on what went wrong. We found out in Ezekiel 28 that he was created 'literally' perfect and that his job was to bring forth the praise to the Almighty God. But that wasn't enough for him; he really wanted to be like God. According to Isaiah 14:12-15, Lucifer says in his heart, *'I will exalt my throne above the stars of God, I will sit also upon the mount of the congregation, in the sides of the north. I will ascend above the heights of the clouds, I will be like the Most High.'* And the rest is history, he was kicked out of heaven and became the one we know today as satan, the wicked and corrupt one, the father of lies.

So let's analyze this, because it will shed light on who we are, and why he hates us so much. He was created to bring forth the praise. Inside of him was the most amazing sounds ever created for the sole purpose of glorifying God. That was his heavenly job description, yet he wanted more...he wanted to literally be like God, his creator. So what he did exactly was to go against what he was created to do, in order to please himself. He introduced selfishness into the universe. As he kept saying, 'I will do this...and I will do this...and I will do this...' it was all about selfishness. Selfishness is the single root to all sin, and the opposite of Gods nature, which is love.

This is important to know, because if you understand that he fell because of selfishness, you understand that's his motivation and how he still gets people to fall to this day. What he does is try to get people to neglect what they were created to do, and get them to focus on themselves. It worked with 1/3 of the heavenly angels, and it has worked with hundreds of millions people since. A person is either motivated by love or selfishness. Which one are you driven by?

Ok, so now we know how he fell, and how he convinces others to fall, but why does he hate us so much? In Genesis, God created the heavens and the earth, the plants, the animals, and everything else. All of these creations came forth out of God, as He spoke them into existence. Yet on the sixth day with man, it is much different. With man he literally forms him out of himself, out of his own image and likeness.

Many of us have read the Genesis verse thousands of times, so it doesn't mean much when we hear 'image and likeness'. Yet if you break that down, image has to do with visual attributes and likeness has to do with the way of being or acting. I used to think that if I saw God, he would be like 300 feet tall and have legs like skyscrapers and hands like mountains. But according to this scripture, and John 14:9-10, God actually looks like you look. In fact, you were created not only to look like him, but to act like him as well. This might offend people who grew up thinking you could never be like God, but that was exactly his intention.

This explains why satan is so mad. It is because he lost everything trying to be what you were created to be. You were created to be in the presence of God, created to be like Him and, have fellowship with Him. Lucifer had just one thought (he couldn't even get it out of his mouth), of trying to be like God, and it was over for him, he was kicked out for all eternity. Wow...talk about a bad case of jealousy. He is a hater, plain and simple, and nobody likes a hater.

As I began to study the believer's authority and our complete authority over sickness, disease, poverty and lack, a tremendous backlash came from all angles. Where did this originate? It is more and more evident that any teaching, or thoughts that are against this originate from the original hater, the devil. We were in fact created to be just like our Father God, and through Jesus we have complete authority over the devil and everything related to him. The first commandment given to man was, 'Be fruitful, and multiply...'

We went through a period of time after Adam sinned when we lost our authority, and became subject to all these horrendous things, such as sickness, poverty, lack, death, etc. Mankind was totally lost. The Bible is the story of God's redemptive love in getting us back to our rightful position.

And now through Jesus, we have the keys to victory, and now have complete authority over the devil and all his devices.

We are now in Christ the reborn sons and daughters of God. Many times when we look at Jesus we see Him as the only son of God, which it says in John 3, but that was before we were born into the family. It might even sound blasphemous to consider that we are in the royal family with Him. However, according to Gal 4:5, we were adopted and have sonship conferred upon us, and are recognized as God's sons. The concept of adoption here is not the unwanted child that is seen as lower in rank than the natural born sons and daughters of the family. No, far from that. In fact, according to Hebrew law, an adopted son has the same equal rights as the firstborn son. And we know who the firstborn son is. So you basically have equal rights to everything that Jesus has, in the heavenly family.

Once you know who you are and the power that has been vested in you, it is all over for the devil and his minions.

6. Who Truly is Called?

That is a serious question. Many Christians never step out and do any miraculous works because somewhere down the line they were convinced that they were not called. I hope to settle this question once and for all. Who truly is called?

Quite simply, if you are reading this article, you are called. One of the greatest revelations I have had since becoming a Christian is that the kingdom of God is like a professional football team holding open try-outs. They put an ad out in the local newspaper, on the radio station, and even a TV ad on ESPN. They announce that anyone who wants to play for us, show up at Lincoln Financial Field, this Saturday at 1:00 pm for a two week try out. The coach even states that even if you cannot play, but would like to play, we will teach you everything you need to know, just show up on Saturday. The potential reach from the advertising is approximately 18 million young men that could play for the team. Of that number, 652 people show up on Saturday. On the first day, the coach explains that all 652 people have the physical ability to make the team, however, each player must follow the specific training instructions to actually make it. Half of the men quit after the first day because it is too hot outside. Day after day, one by one, people quit the team for various reasons, until at the end of the two weeks, the roster was down to just 81 players. 18 Million men could have made the team, but only 81 will actually be playing for the team.

The Kingdom of God is the same way. Many are called, but the chosen are few. Millions of people are called to do the amazing, miraculous works of Jesus. There is an open invitation to all. God is no respecter of persons. The people who are chosen are simply the ones who actually show up. After that, the ones who go onto perfection are the ones who are faithful to that calling, seeking His face with all their heart every day.

This might be too simple for most to grasp, but this is what Jesus was trying to explain to James and John's mother in Matthew 20 when she asked if they could sit at the right hand and the left hand of Jesus. He replied that it is not up to him to give, but to those who it is prepared of by the Father. In other words, how great or how small you become in the kingdom is not really up to Jesus, it's up to what cost you are willing to pay; and only the Father knows beforehand where you will actually end up. Will you be a general in the kingdom, leading multitudes from various nations to Christ, or will you backslide and totally renounce Him? That is up to you.

The church has it backwards. In most churches, the Pastor is the superstar—praying for the sick, leading people to Christ, etc., and the members just watch Sunday after Sunday and never really do anything. According to Ephesians 4:11, the five offices of church leadership are: apostle, prophet, evangelist, pastor, and teacher. Their role is to equip the body of Christ (church members) to do the work of the ministry. The church leadership should serve more along the lines of coaches, and the members should be doing the work of laying hands on the sick, reaching the lost, casting out demons, etc. Mike Brown (coach of the Los Angeles Lakers), is not supposed to be on the court making all the shots, getting rebounds, and blocking shots. It's just not his role.

I think most Christians are not doing the works, because they truly do not understand how powerful they really are. According to 2 Corinthians 1:21, you have been anointed by God. You are just as much anointed as the most 'powerful' Pastor you see on TV, or any other believer in the world, even as anointed as Jesus. Hopefully you did not choke on that statement, but the same Spirit that raised Jesus from the dead, lives in you. **He does the works through you**.

An analogy of this can be illustrated in the Old Testament. In the days of Moses, the children of Israel did not really have to do anything. Moses would go hear from God, wave his staff and BOOM... the people would get delivered. He was like Superman, and everyone else was just mere men, having no clue what was going on. He knew God's ways, and they only saw God's acts. Ultimately, this got them nowhere. He was frustrated because they would complain all the time, they were lost in the wilderness, and never made it into the promised land.

Later Joshua comes along with a different style of management. He had the same instructions as Moses, yet he had totally different results. With Joshua it was understood that if they are going to claim victory and take this promised land, they are going to have to win as a team. Everyone must fight.

In the same way, the great and mighty men of God of the 19th and 20th century did many amazing things in the Spirit. Tongues were re-introduced on a grand scale. Healing meetings where thousands were healed in tent revival meetings took place. Yet the church as a whole is not in any better shape today than it was 100 years ago. Why is this?

In the 1900s those mighty men of God could be like Moses and perform miracles without the assistance of the members in the pews. However, if we are to see the mass worldwide revival , we must be like Joshua and understand that this move of God only takes place when we **all** get involved. Take a stand today to be bold in faith and do the works of Jesus.

Here is one more example of what it is going to take to spark mass revival. Remember the story in Matt 14, when Peter sees Jesus on the water and decides to walk out to Him? Just imagine if the other disciples in the boat got stirred up and decided to get out too, and all the disciples were stepping out and running on the water! Now imagine what kind of effect that would have on the people on the shore, as these men are running out to them from the sea, without a boat! Would they have to do much explaining of the kingdom of God? No, because they just demonstrated it.

7. Hearing from God- Was that from Me, God, or the Devil?

Probably the most frequently asked question I receive is, 'How can I hear the voice of God?' This question is typically followed by, 'Was that thought from me, God, or the devil?' Discerning God's voice can be the difference between life and death, wealth or poverty, healing or sickness.

Hearing the voice of God is probably the most important tool we have as believers. How can we obey God if we do not know what he is saying to us? Hearing from God is not optional, we are expected to hear his voice. Jesus said, 'My sheep hear my voice, and a stranger's voice, they will not follow'. How good of an employee would you be, if you could never hear your boss' voice?

First, let's tackle the topic of discussion, 'me, God, or the devil'. This is actually a question of mind renewal. Mind renewal, according to Romans 12:1-2, is the degree to which, one's mind has been transformed from the fallen, sinful state to the mind of Christ. When we first received Christ and became born again, our Spirit became brand new; yet our mind and body did not change. Spiritually speaking, we were made to be identical twins of Jesus the moment we received him as Savior. Everything He was able to do on the earth, we are able to do; immediately. So why don't we? You don't *think* you can. Your mind, or soul, is in the way. Your mind, or soul, is the filter through which you see the world.

The accuracy to which you are able to hear God's voice is based upon the degree to which your mind is renewed to God's Word.

Let me use an illustration. I was watching the Cowboys and Dolphins game yesterday for Thanksgiving, when I received a phone call. I reached for my remote to turn down the volume, so I could hear the person on the other end. However, the volume did not go down. Frustrated, I told the person I would call them back and put in new batteries in my remote. Same thing happened, no response to the TV. I couldn't change the channel or anything. What was going on? I became very frustrated and was about to call Customer Care when I realized that a book on my TV stand was blocking the TV sensor (which allows the remote to communicate to the TV). I removed the book and everything started working fine again. This is how many Christians are. God is sending direct messages to us, yet many don't receive them because there is something blocking the signal. So they become frustrated, and instead of removing what is blocking the signal, they do all kinds of silly things that never work.

Romans 12:1-2 gives us instructions on how to renew our minds. Present your body to God, and do not be conformed to the world's system, so that you can hear God and discern His will for your life. An unrenewed mind is going to think in line with what the world thinks. If the world thinks sex outside of marriage is ok, then you think sex outside of marriage is ok. If the world thinks the economy is getting worse, then you start to pull back and prepare to downsize. Your mind is shaped by what you see and hear. In Mark 4:24, Jesus says to be careful of what you are hearing, because the measure of thought and study you give to a subject is the extent to which it will show up in your life. What does He mean by that? He means that if you watch reality TV for 5 hours a day and read the Bible for 10 minutes, the thought patterns in line with that reality TV show will be more prevalent in your life than the 10 minutes of Bible study.

Don't be fooled, the messages that come through watching television are not in line with the Word of God. According to Nielson, the average American household watches 35 hours of television a week! So for us to renew our minds to the Word, we must resist the temptation to conform to the world and stay in the Word. Keep the Word always present before you. Study it, read it, and meditate on it (those are 3 different things). The more you spend time with it, the more you will *want* to spend more time with it. This is how you renew your mind, and a renewed mind receives the Jesus-type of results.

So back to our original question? Is it Me, God, or the devil? If your mind is 100% renewed and the signal is pure, what you say and what you are hearing will line up with what God says. Also, the devil, who is a thief, and a liar, will become totally exposed. The devil's thoughts are always based in fear, negativity or selfishness. What do I mean by having a pure signal? A pure signal does not have anything blocking the receiver. In short, living a holy life is vital. Nothing can twist up your signal worse than living in sin and unforgiveness (which also is sin). Sin destroys your boldness and confidence towards the things God says, and instead adds condemnation to the mix. It gives the devil something to talk to you about. So disconnect that evil line of communication by repenting from sin, rebuke the condemnation, and walk boldly in the confidence that God speaks directly to you.

Have you received a thought or idea that was so big, you are not sure what to do? What if you received a big thought about moving, accepting a new job, or opening up a business? Here is a basic checklist to know if what you have heard came from God:

1. You can find it in the Word of God. God never contradicts his Word. Ever
2. It takes faith to accomplish it. God tends to give us ideas about big things, and this thing is *so* big, you know you couldn't have thought about this on your own.
3. The world and the unsaved probably think you are crazy. They are not in agreement with it all.
4. It will take courage to do it
5. You have a peace about it.

8. The Prophetic vs. The Psychic

Yes, God still speaks. And He has some pretty good things to say to you, you should really spend some time with Him.

I was recently entertaining some friends over at my place when suddenly I felt impressed to give a prophetic word to one of them. She received the word, as it brought her to tears; however she made references later about it being some sort of psychic experience. I realized then and there that so many people do not understand the clear differences between the psychic and the prophetic realm. And there are **clear** differences.

There are 3 main differences between the psychic realm and the prophetic realm. Knowing these can save you from being exposed to unclean spirits and certain bondages that can cling to you if you allow them. Let's explore these differences based on what the Bible has to say.

The first and most important difference is the source. A psychic, medium, tarot card reader, spirit guide, soothsayer, or sorcerer is relying on a source for its information. They are pulling information from the spirit realm from such entities as demonic spirits or familiar spirits. These familiar spirits have been around for thousands of years and probably have even been around your family for many years, so they know intimate things about you. Hence the name, 'familiar' spirit. An example of this is when someone claims to be speaking to the dead, they are actually speaking to that familiar spirit that knew the deceased individual and the family.

The source for the prophetic realm is **solely** the Holy Spirit.

Ok, that all makes sense, but what if you cannot discern the source? Well here is the second difference which should clearly identify the source. Direction. Which direction is it leading you? A psychic is going to lead you inward, where a prophet is going to point you to the cross. A true prophetic word will give you the sense that you are sitting right in the throne room talking directly to Jesus. You will be overflowing with the love of God, and it will be hard to contain yourself. After you receive a true prophetic word, you will want to run to Jesus and follow Him even the more. However a message from a psychic will be focused on you and only you. If it doesn't make you feel like running to Jesus, but is only about you, chances are it did not come from heaven.

The third major distinction is motive. Did you have to pay to receive a word? Did you call a 900 number or respond to an advertisement and pay an upfront fee? This is a major red flag, as Jesus commanded us to freely give, as we have freely received. To be clear, many have started out pure and holy but have been seduced by the dark side and now no longer represent God. An example of this is the prophet Balaam in the book of Numbers. He was a former prophet who was seduced (by money) by Balak to say a negative word and curse the children of Israel. Motive is always a clear way to find out if someone is operating in line with heaven. The motive for a genuine prophetic word is simply to move a person to be closer to Christ and His will for their life. Avoid those who have a compromised motive.

Accuracy, it should be noted, is not a deciding factor in determining the source of a message. A psychic or medium can be extremely accurate, and lead you right into destruction. In Acts 16, a medium cried out many days after Paul and his men, 'These men are servants of the Most High God, to show us the way of salvation.' Was she accurate? Yes, she was very accurate, yet she was still operating from a source other than the Holy Spirit, and Paul discerned it and cast that divination spirit out of her.

The Bible clearly forbids us from consulting with psychics, mediums, and soothsayers. Yet many Christians go see them on a regular basis. Why does God forbid this? Isn't it harmless to just call up the psychic hotline? When you consult a psychic, you open yourself up to the spirit that is behind that psychic. If a lust spirit or depression spirit is behind that tarot card reader, you are directly connecting with that spirit. In fact, the very act of consulting with it, gives it legal permission to enter into your life. Many find themselves in bondage to lust, addiction, gluttony and cannot seem to figure out why. This is why in Exodus 22 and Leviticus 20, God commands those that dabble in this type of witchcraft and sorcery to be put to death. Still seem harmless?

God does still speak today, and hearing from Him is still as amazing as it was in the Bible days. In fact every human being is born with a desire to hear what He has to say. Yet many churches today teach that He no longer speaks to us. So where do they go to satisfy this innate desire? That's right, they settle and go visit a psychic.

Don't settle for the counterfeit. God wants to speak to you directly. Will you let Him?

9. The Secret Key to Prophesying Accurately

This past year I had the pleasure of being invited to a prophetic conference in North Georgia, and I suddenly realized that I get asked many of the same questions wherever I go concerning prophecy. So I figured I would share the secret key to being able to prophesy effectively and accurately. First of all, every Christian should prophesy. That's right, I said every Christian. You have the ability, as the Holy Spirit is with you, and Paul says it over and over again in 1 Corinthians 14.

Now when I speak about prophesying, I'm not referring to you going up to someone, and telling them that within 5 days destruction in the form of a tornado is coming to their home. Nor am I talking about endtime prophecy, where we all try to guess who the antichrist is and when the rapture will take place. My desire is to 'demystify' prophesying and show you in a clear and concise way how it can be used to win people to Christ. To put it simply, to prophesy means to encourage, uplift, or exhort. Everything else in not prophesying, no matter how amazing it sounds or how accurate it is, if it does not encourage, uplift, or exhort. Now while you are prophesying, other gifts can be activated such as a word of knowledge (in which you suddenly know a key detail about a person's past or present), a word of wisdom (a detail about a person's future) or several of the other gifts of the Spirit. But I want to focus on the fact that it must encourage, uplift, or exhort. I never focus on the 'gifts' when I minister to people, as in is it this gift or that gift; I'll let them debate that in seminary school or theology papers. I just flow in the Spirit. Unfortunately many people never step out because they feel they don't have this gift or that gift, when in actuality, if you have the Holy Spirit you have everything you need.

Focusing on the gifts is like focusing on the leather seats, or power steering, or a certain type of engine of car. No, if you purchase the car, all of those features come with the car. If you are filled with the Holy Spirit, everything He has, you now have. Jesus did not possess any ability while on earth that you don't have access to, thru the power of the Holy Spirit. People try to pick and choose gifts like it is some sort of spiritual buffet line or salad bar. Now some might feel more comfortable in the area of healing or in the area of prophecy because they have spent more time in that area, but if you step out by faith in areas you have not traditionally spent time in, you will become more balanced and be able to trust God in those new areas.

Now back to the secret key to being able to prophesy effectively and accurately. It is very possible that you can deliver a prophetic word to someone and it is as if Jesus himself was right there giving it to them, and transform their life forever. Someone can go from being suicidal, to feeling totally victorious all with a prophetic utterance from the Lord. So how is this possible? How do you hear key intimate details about someone, that only them and God know? The answer is so simple you could stumble over it. It all works by love.

As you are filled with the love of God, it will cause you to share this love with others. Love them to such an extent that all you want to do is encourage, uplift, and exhort them. So how did Jesus move? How was he motivated? Over and over, throughout the gospels, as he was ministering to people, it would say he was moved with 'compassion'. That is the secret key. Compassion is 'love in action'.

Most people are afraid to prophecy to people because they think they will get it wrong. They are afraid they will 'mis-hear' something and then the person will look at them like they are stupid or crazy. This mentality is 100% wrong because instead of thinking about the other person, you are concerned only about yourself, rooted in selfishness (the direct opposite of love). However if you focus on them, loving them, and blessing them, and being an encouragement to them, you will **never** be wrong.

And as you love as Christ loves them, the Holy Spirit will begin to give you words of knowledge and other gifts so that you can more effectively minister to them. Always know that it is never about you, it is always about them. An easy way to spot the enemy is if you hear, *'what if...'*.(what if I heard incorrectly, what if they don't receive what I'm saying, what if I lay hands and it doesn't work, etc) This is always his attempt to get you to focus on yourself instead of the one needing ministering.

So when I was at the prophetic conference, in one session while I was prophesying to people for about 2 hours straight, the love of God rushed in and completely overwhelmed me. It was as if God allowed me to share His heart, to see the people as He saw them. I didn't care how accurate I was about the words of knowledge, if they received what I said or if they would do something about the prophetic words they were receiving. All I cared about was loving them, encouraging them, and uplifting them. This is how Jesus sees people.

Moving by compassion and focusing on love is the secret key to prophecy. God loves people **so** much, and as you tap into that love, you will find yourself flowing in the Spirit as you never have before, hearing things you never heard before, and operating on a level that totally baffles the world. That is why Paul is able to say, Love never fails.

Here are some easy points to remember:

1. Be moved with compassion

*2. It's **NOT** about you*

3. Encourage, uplift, exhort

4. Practice Practice Practice (the more you practice, the more confident you will become and you will be able to clearly hear what the Holy Spirit is saying)

5. Protect your hearing (if you are listening to ungoldly radio and TV all day you will not have the confidence that what you are hearing is of God, it is contaminating your spirit) Stay in the Word!

6. Don't be afraid to take risks! (As you grow, don't be afraid stretch out and give names or places the Holy Spirit will give you as you are ministering)

God wants to reach out to people far more than we allow Him to. There are probably only a handful of people out there that truly 'go into all the world', so when someone steps out, heaven is going to back you 100%. Stop having fear of yourself and allow the Holy Spirit to totally use you, He has been waiting on you, and the people have been waiting for you.

10. The Nutritional Value of the Word

Did you know that everything edible is not actually food? Just because your body can digest something, does not mean that it has any nutritional value to your body. For example, you can get 'full' off eating twinkies and Krispy Kreme donuts, but that doesn't mean your body received any nutritional value at all. Hang in there with me while I prove this point. Your mind tells your body that it is full, however, your body says it hasn't received anything (of nutritional value). So what does your body do? It stores up extra because it thinks that it is starving. This is how people become fat and obese.

Everything you see, hear, or read, does not have (nutritional) value to your spirit. The only thing that is 100% spiritual value to your spirit is the Word of God. It will nourish your spirit, replenish your body, and renew your mind. The pure Word of God is rare and hard to find in today's society. Most people would rather watch Christian television or pick up a spiritual book as a shortcut. In the same example I used above in which you could eat junk food and convince your body that it is full, people everyday do the same thing spiritually. They watch hours of television and fill their spirit with meaningless junk. If you ate a gallon of Ben and Jerry's ice cream, you would have no room for spinach. In the same way, if you watched 3 movies back to back, you would have no room for Corinthians. Even if your mind cannot register it, your body craves spinach, its nutrients give it energy and rejuvenation , and life. Your spirit craves the Word. It needs the Word to live, for faith, to resist the devil, and more. The Word gives you insight and instruction when your mind does not know what to do or what decision to make. Are you a spiritually obese Christian today?

An obese person cannot do the things an athlete in top physical condition can do. They lack the energy, ability, and stamina to carry out certain tasks. Not because they don't want to, but because of all the excess fat that they are carrying. In the same way, a spiritually obese person cannot do certain things that God has commanded them to do because of all the excess F.A.T (feelings, attitudes, and thoughts) that they have accumulated through television, magazines, movies, internet. They know they are supposed to pray daily, win the lost, love their neighbor, and read the Bible, but their F.A.T . will not let them.

So how do you become spiritually fit? Do everything in your power to have your feelings, attitudes, and thoughts, line up directly with God's Word. Reject those things that contradict the Word. The biggest deception that the devil uses is to mix 99% truth with 1% lie. It seems and sounds true and correct, but that 1% will kill you. Just ask Eve, everything the serpent told her was not a lie, but the part that was a lie, led to her destruction. Everyone that the devil has deceived over the past 6000+ years fell because they believed the 99% truth he spoke, and digested the 1% lie as well. It only takes one drop of rat poison to kill you, and in the spirit it only takes the 1% lie to make you spiritually obese and render you ineffective.

As I mentioned in an earlier post, the Word of God is pure nutrition for your spirit. But if we dig a little deeper, we can discover just how truly Jesus drove home this point. Several times throughout the gospels, Jesus made reference to his body as 'the bread come down from heaven' and said that whosoever eats his body and drinks his flesh has eternal life (John 6). What is he referring to? Cannibalism?

This was a hard message for his disciples to grasp, for they did not really understand who He was. According to John 1:1, Jesus is not just the Son of God, but He is literally the Word of God. The point that Jesus was trying to drive home is that we need to eat him (the Word) daily for our sustenance. His Word is the lifeline we need just like food is needed for the body.

Still not convinced? Check out this illustration. Jesus was born in Bethlehem in a manger. I am sure you have seen the Christmas stories with the nativity scenes and the wisemen, etc. Yet, most people completely miss the underlying meaning behind it.

Everything in scripture has meaning, nothing just happens. Jesus could have been born anywhere, why a manger? What exactly is a manger anyway? I'm a city guy from New Jersey, so I had no clue what a manger is, as I'm sure most people reading this have no clue. A manger is a feeding trough, where the animals (sheep) would come to get their food. Jesus was born in this feeding trough, layed in swaddling clothes for everyone to see. From his birth it is evident that we are supposed to feed off of his flesh (the Word) just as the sheep feed off the trough (manger).

I bet you never heard that analogy in your child's Christmas play.

Jesus, or the Word of God, is to be highly valued and never taken lightly. It is our protection. In John 6, Jesus referred to himself as the 'bread come down from heaven' (translated manna). Recall in Numbers 21 when the children of Israel began to despise the manna they were receiving daily. As they began to complain, fiery snakes came out of the forest and bit and killed many Israelites that day. Where did those fiery snakes come from? Those snakes were always there in the wilderness. But once they began to despise (think little of) their manna from heaven, they lost their protection from God, allowing the snakes to have an all you can eat buffet on them. In the same way, once you begin to lose sight of the Word of God, and think of it in little regard, you give the enemy permission to have an all you can eat buffet on you too! It is your protection, never forget that.

If you have taken the Word lightly, there is hope for you today. In Numbers 21:7, as the people were being destroyed by the serpents, God instructed Moses to create a brass serpent and put it on a pole. And any man who had been bitten, if he looked upon that brass serpent, he would be healed. Well today we have a more sure word of assurance than that brass serpent that Moses created. We have the Word which became flesh and died for our sins. And any man that has been bitten in any way by the devil can be totally set free, by believing on His name. Christ is our redemption and hope of glory! Hallelujah!

I think I just typed myself happy! Praise Him!

11. Let's Talk About Faith

Faith is one of the most misunderstood words in the English language. Usually when someone says faith, they mean believe. What is your faith? And someone would respond, *I'm a Baptist, or I'm Jewish or Catholic.* But true Bible faith is actually much deeper than that. Whenever the disciples would ask Jesus how he was able to perform miracles, or why they were not able to, he would always respond by telling them it is because of their faith. (or the lack thereof).

Faith is **the** most powerful force in the universe. By faith the world was created, men and woman came back to life, and individuals received divine healing (Hebrews 11). Faith is the system that God uses whenever he wants to do something, so it is very important that we understand it. In fact, in that same chapter in Hebrews it says that it is impossible to please God without faith. In 4 different places in the Bible, it says, *'the just shall live by faith.'* So how can you live by faith if you don't know what it is? Lets explore this mighty topic.

Faith is the currency of the universe. That is the best analogy I can use to describe what faith is; it is like spiritual money. Lets dig deeper into this analogy. There is not a whole lot that I can do with 25 one hundred dollar bills. I can use it as a paper weight or a door stop, or even fold them up and make decorations with them, but they are just pieces of paper. However, the power of these pieces of paper come from what they represent and what I can exchange them for. I can exchange them for a car, a TV , or even a new living room set. In fact, if you had enough of these pieces of paper, there is basically nothing that you cannot have. Imagine for one second if you had 10 billion dollars worth of these pieces of paper, how powerful would you be?

Now keeping that illustration in mind, faith is the same concept as money. In Hebrews 11, it is defined as the substance of things hoped for, the evidence of things not seen. So faith is not 'hoping' or 'wishful thinking.' It is an actual substance, even if it not tangible with your natural eyes. Faith is the vehicle which brings those things which are in the spiritual world, into this natural world. The Bible is full of promises from God, from financial prosperity, to healing, to family restoration. What brings these promises into your life is faith. Without faith, you will not partake in any of these promises, you will just observe them from afar, and then make up some weird doctrine about why you cannot receive from God.

Just like with money, if you have 50 dollars, you cannot realistically expect to purchase a Ferrari, it's going to take more cash. Well if you have never used faith ever in your life, and you expect to beat a giant like AIDS or a million dollar debt supernaturally cancelled, it's probably not going to work for you, you need more 'spiritual cash'. The good news is that Jesus said it doesn't take much, 'if you had faith the size of a mustard seed...' . Begin to build up your faith. Use your faith to overcome a cold, or a headache or to pay a bill, and slowly build up to the 'big stuff'. The rate you go is entirely up to you. Faith is all about trust in God. It all about relationship. It's not that you cannot defeat cancer or AIDS as a beginner, it's just that you have not developed that trust relationship with God yet, so you are not fully convinced it will work for you. After you have seen a headache defeated a few times, you become confident that a headache must be defeated when you command it to.

God never intended us to live *normal* lives. Step out on faith and begin living a supernatural life, living by faith just as Jesus did. Rely on this to provide your healing and your financial independence.

You might start slow, but start today... your destiny awaits.

12. Faith vs Belief

Many people confuse faith with belief. These are two totally separate things. Belief is a state of mind, while faith is an act, based upon that mindset. The reason why most Christians do not see the promises of God (healing, financial prosperity, happy relationships, etc.) is because they honestly believe, but they do not apply faith. It is good to believe, and you must believe, but it is faith that activates these blessings and makes them a reality for ***you***.

Here is an illustration about the difference between faith and belief. A man is walking through the Arabian desert during the heat of the day while it is about 100 degrees. He has not drunk any water, so his body is beginning to dehydrate. A stranger walks by him and gives him a bottle of water. He is thankful for the water, because he is incredibly thirsty and is about to pass out. This man believes that if he drinks the water, he will not pass out. He is so happy that someone came and gave him water that he starts rejoicing. He pulls out his cell phone and calls his wife saying, *'I'm not going to pass out, because a stranger just gave me water.'* Then he calls his mother and is rejoicing saying, *'I have been saved from my dehydration, I shall not die.'* Then he calls his best friend and says, *'I am truly favored, a stranger just came up to me and gave me*—before he could finish his sentence, he passes out. He never got around to actually drinking the water. He believed, but had no faith (action).

This is a clear representation of the church of 2012. It's not that people do not believe the promises of God, most genuinely do. They just do the same thing as this guy walking around the desert. A preacher will declare to them God's promises and all throughout the congregation the people will shout and run up and down the aisles, slap their neighbor and spin around. But what they do not realize is if they just believe the Word and do not **act** upon it, they will not see any fruit of the Word in their lives. That's why in most churches across the United States, the majority of the congregation is sick, broke, in debt, divorced, or just miserable. In Hebrews 4:2 it says that the Word preached did not profit the people because they did not mix it with faith. Be a doer of the Word, and not a hearer only, deceiving yourself.

Messages about faith are being preached Sunday after Sunday. But we as Christians are not called to know about faith and teach faith, we are called to **do** our faith, and **live** by our faith. It is almost as if the average Christian Pastor can tell what you what faith is, how to get faith, the benefits of faith, but cannot tell you the last time he used faith. Jesus asks in Luke 18:8, when the Son of Man comes back, will he find faith on the earth? I don't know if he will, but he certainly will find plenty of books, CDs and conferences about it.

Just go ahead and DRINK the water already.

13. Hope: The Starting point of Faith

A clear understanding of faith is vital to every Christian believer. It is spoken about countless times throughout the New Testament, to the point where Hebrews 11:6 states that you cannot even please God without it. Four times we are instructed to *walk by faith*. So what is faith and how do we 'walk by faith?' This might seem pretty basic, but it really is not. It is very simple, yet it is not easy to live a life of faith. For example, all throughout the Bible, stories of faith are illustrated, examples are given, yet there is only one chapter in the whole Bible that details the people who actually lived by it. (Hebrews 11). Over a period of about 4,000 years only about a handful of people actually lived by faith.

I don't think it was intended to be very complicated. I'm sure you can find a 16 CD series on faith, or a 600 page book on the subject, but I'm going to make it so simple a 5 year old can grasp it. As I've stated in earlier, faith is the most powerful force in the universe. Through it the worlds were framed, animals created, bodies healed, debts cancelled, etc. However you cannot isolate faith. Faith is not intended to work by itself. It can only work with hope and love, its two siblings. Hope probably gets the least amount of publicity of the trio. So in order to fully understand the concept of faith, we will discuss hope.

In no way is hope any less powerful than faith or love. In fact, you could argue that it is the most powerful. The hope that I am describing is not the traditional concept of hope. The traditional view of hope is synonymous to wishful thinking. I am *'hoping and praying'* that I get healed. I am *'hoping and praying'* I get that bill paid. The traditional view of hope is very similar to the traditional concept of prayer, but that's a whole different topic.

Everything begins with hope. Without hope there is no faith, there is no victory, there is nothing. Hope can be defined as joyful expectation based on a promise given to you by God. It is rooted in the Word of God and revealed to you either by the written Word of God, a spoken word directly from God, a vision, a sermon, a book (like this one), or about 50 other ways that God can speak to you. The focus however is the Word of God; it cannot contradict what is written. You cannot have biblical hope that a man you find is physically attractive will leave his wife and be with you, that is opposite the Word.

Biblical hope must remain alive. I remember a phrase Jesse Jackson used to say, 'Keep Hope Alive'; nothing could be more true than that statement. Your hope, or your joyful expectation, will ignite your faith. Before faith can kick in, you must have a clear picture of what you expect. Give your mind and spirit something to work with. For example, you have just contracted some form of sickness and you decide to use these concepts of hope, faith, and love to overcome. Even though this example is for healing, the concept works in all scenarios.

First begin with developing your hope. Through the Word, you know that you have a divine right for your body to be healed. Get out every scripture you can pertaining to divine healing, write them down and keep them always present before your eyes. Now you are beginning to get excited, because you are building up your hope, your joyful expectation. You are developing a clear picture what God has said to you, that He would heal you, and now you are filled with joy and expectation. Literally see yourself (in your imagination) completely healed. That is hope.

On a sidenote, biblical hope employs the use of your imagination. Imagination is a tool given to us, that very few believers actually put to use. Usually when most people think of imagination, we think of bad stuff like sexual perversion, but this is a God-given tool, that is to be used to 'see' things before they actually occur. Society tells children to quit imagining things at a young age, so by the time we are adults, this gift is usually turned off, and needs to be developed again. Train your imagination to 'see' in the Spirit those things which have been freely given to us by God. People may think you are crazy, but your amazing results will prove otherwise.

Faith brings what you 'hope' into the natural realm from the 'imagined' or spirit world to make it a reality; but it all starts with hope. A joyful expectation of what God spoke to you. How do you develop hope? Where does it actually come from? Well, it doesn't come from you. You didn't make this stuff up. Take time each day to spend in God's presence. He will speak to you in the form of ideas, witty concepts; things that are way bigger than you. Take time to search the scriptures for promises he spoke directly to you thousands of years ago and allow Him to illuminate their hidden value to you.

Everything starts with hope.

14. Simplifying the Gifts of the Spirit

When I first received Jesus as Savior I can recall sitting in the congregation of my church and watching the Pastor lay hands on the people who came to the altar to receive healing. As they were getting healed, I would think to myself, *'wow, that gift of healing is amazing, I sure wish I had that gift.'* Yet because I didn't have that gift (or so I thought), I would just sit in the pew week after week, while people all over the city were sick. Then a few months later, a visiting prophet came to our church, and astounded our congregation with accurate words of knowledge and encouraging prophetic words. So I thought to myself, *'wow, his gift is truly amazing, imagine what is must be like to have a gift like that!'* Yet because I didn't have the prophetic gift (or so I thought), I would sit in the pew week after week while hundreds of people around me were lonely, sad, and depressed, needing a word of encouragement.

Traditionally we have been taught that only the select few, spiritual elite can possess a spiritual gift. Someone like a Pastor or Bishop or Evangelist can have a gift of healing or miracles while the laypeople just go to church and watch them perform. Is this the blueprint of the New Testament?

We come to church and are entertained by the person on stage, while we sit just there? This sounds more like an R&B concert than biblical Christianity.

During the charismatic revival of the 1970's, the gifts of the Spirit really hit the forefront of the Christian scene. It was during this time, prophecy, healing, and miracles, really went mainstream, being displayed in large churches, on radio, and broadcast on television. This is all based upon 1 Corinthians 12, which lists the 9 gifts of the Spirit: 3 are speaking gifts (prophecy, tongues, interpretation of tongues), 3 are revelation gifts (discernment, word of knowledge, word of wisdom), and 3 are power gifts (faith, healing, miracles).

Outside of 1 Corinthians 12-14, there is very little mention of spiritual gifts in the New Testament. Did Jesus ever teach about the gifts? The problem with the 'gift' teaching is that, how do you know if you have a spiritual gift? And if you don't have a particular gift, then what do you do? Because I didn't think I had the gift of healing, I would pass on people in my midst that I know needed healing. The traditional view of this teaching is that one person has a prophetic gift, another person has a gift of miracles, and another gets Words of knowledge, and someone else can interpret tongues. *This is flat out wrong*, and leads many people to just do nothing, because they are convinced they have not been equipped with a certain gift. I should know, because I was one of those people.

The true Bible teaching is that if you possess the Holy Spirit, that is the only gift you need. The Holy Spirit will allow you to meet the needs of anyone you come across at any time. If you come across a lady who has the bird flu, you don't need to go run and find Bishop Apostle Rev. E.T. White, IV, you are fully equipped to lay hands and administer healing on the spot. The same thing goes with prophecy, and everything else. **The Holy Spirit disperses the gifts as you need them.**

When I had this revelation, that because I possess the Holy Spirit, I have access to all 9 gifts of the Spirit, I began to run with it. At the grocery store, when I saw a man with a sling on his arm, I laid hands on him to be healed. I began to give prophetic words to strangers and watch the Holy Spirit pour over them. I was truly on fire for God and began to demonstrate the kingdom of God wherever I went! This is the true meaning of *operating in the Spirit.* You have been given the authority to demonstrate the kingdom of God wherever your feet tread upon. The key is to not focus on possessing this gift or that gift, focus on the need of the person standing in front of you, and the Holy Spirit will do all the rest.

Now let's put 1 Corinthians back into perspective. The Corinthian church was a carnal church, they had all types of sin running rampant in the church, yet they still had these gifts operating in their midst. So for clarity, the Apostle Paul explains what these gifts were and how they work. Yet in the last verse of chapter 12, explaining these gifts he says, 'yet I show unto you a more excellent way'. **This is the way I am showing you**. The very next chapter, I Corinthians 13 is known as the love chapter. Love is the secret key that actually unlocks all of these gifts. This is how Jesus did it. He was moved with compassion to heal people. Compassion is love in action. As you see people around you, in need of healing, an encouraging word, a financial need, or anything, you will have so much compassion it will move you to do something.

It's not about you. It's not about your gift. It's all about the needs of the people, and God using you to minister to them.

15. Can Everyone Be Healed?

Before we answer this question, I have a question for you. Do you believe the Bible is the Truth and the infallible Word of God? I mean, *do you really believe* it? If the answer to that question is no, then nothing in this section or any sermon concerning healing or miracles will make any sense to you and you will probably be mad by the time you finish reading. If you answer yes to that question then I have some exciting news for you.

Because of our sins we have been made susceptible to the curse on the earth. The results of this curse are death, sickness, poverty, demonic oppression, depression, etc. Not only that, we were separated from God, and condemned to an eternal existence apart from Him in heaven. Just when everything looked hopeless on earth, around 2000 years ago, Jesus, the Son of God, came down to the earth, and paid the price for our sins (by being crucified on the cross and raising up from the dead), so now we can be made right with God. So what does this exactly mean? According to John 3:16, God so loved the world, that He sent his only begotten son, that whosoever believes in Him, will not perish, but have everlasting life. In another scripture it says, If you confess with your mouth the Lord Jesus, and shalt believe in your heart that God raised him from the dead, you shall be saved (Romans 10:9)

So if I believe in my heart that Jesus is Lord, and confess it with my mouth, then I am saved, or born again. I believe this because the Bible says that is the way it is. Are there situations in which if someone believes in their heart and confess with their mouth that they will not be saved? Not according to scripture. It does not matter how evil the person is, or what bad thing they have done, Jesus will save all that come to him in this way. Romans 10:9 gives the blueprint for how to be saved: 1) Believe in your heart and 2)confess with your mouth. If you really believe in your heart, but never say anything, according to this scripture, you are not saved. Also, if you confessed out of your mouth, but never really believed it in your heart, you are not saved.

That same blueprint in Romans 10:9 on how to become born again, is the same blueprint to receive all the promises of God. They are all given by grace freely, but we access them by faith. One of these promises, healing, is a right to every believer in Jesus. So how do you use your faith to receive your healing? According to Romans 10:9, the first step is to believe it in your heart. But what are you believing? Just because you know you have a divine right to healing will not get you healed. And just because the preacher just prayed for the lady standing next to you and she got healed, will not necessarily get **you** healed. Even if you *really* want God to heal you, that will not get you healed. The only thing that moves God is faith, so that is what is going to get you healed. And we know that faith is based upon the Word of God. So first you must consume your heart with what He said concerning healing. He said:

Who his self bare our sins in his own body on the tree, that we, being dead to sins, should live unto righteousness: by whose stripes you were healed - (1 Peter 2:24)

And said, If thou wilt hearken to the voice of the Lord thy God, and wilt do that which is right in his sight, and wilt give ear to his commandments, and keep all his statues, I will put none of these diseases upon thee, which I have brought upon the Egyptians, for I am the Lord that healeth thee. (Exodus 15:26)

And these signs shall follow them that believe... they shall lay hands on the sick, and they shall recover (Mark 16:17-18)

But he was wounded for our transgressions, he was bruised for our iniquities: the chastisement of our peace was upon him; and with his stripes we are healed (Isa 53:5)

These are just a few of the scriptures in the Bible concerning healing, there are many more. You do not need to know 15 scriptures concerning healing, attend healing conferences all around the world, and take a theology class on divine healing for the healing power of God to work in your life. You just have to understand that it is in fact God's will to heal, just as it is God's will to save souls. There is not one instance in the New Testament where someone came to Jesus for healing and he turned them down. So take time to become familiar with these healing scriptures, meditate on them until you believe them with all your heart. Do you believe them? Do you take God at His Word when he said by his stripes you **were** healed? If you cannot believe his stripes have paid the price for your healing in 1 Peter 2:24 and Isa 53:5, can you truly believe Jesus paid the price for your sins in John 3:16 and Romans 10:9? This is a serious point of reflection as you ask yourself, *can God's Word be trusted?* (That's why I asked that in the beginning of the section.)

So now let's say you believe it with all your heart, and you have biblical hope concerning healing. Hope is great, but only faith is what releases the miracle. Faith is acting upon that which you believe (the Word), and fully expecting the desired result (of the Word). Faith is an action word, your faith can be seen in you doing something (based upon the Word). We believe therefore we speak (2 Cor 4:13) For an example of faith, because I believe that Jesus was beaten so that my body could be healed, I speak directly to whatever is not acting right, and command it to be healed in Jesus name. Be aggressive with it, you have a divine right to healing, in Mark 11, Jesus spoke directly to a fig tree.

By implementing the principles of faith, based upon the Word of God, you can be healed, no matter the circumstance. Healing always comes. It might not always come instantly, but you have to stand for what you say you believe. Be open to hear specific words from God such as 'stretch out your right hand' or 'call Jennifer and forgive her'. Obeying his specific instructions are a part of you releasing your faith. Just like Jesus desires all to be saved, he desires all to be healed. Release your faith and watch the healing power of God flow through you today!

16. Focus On the Mission, and Stop trying to Predict His Return

Every few years a prediction arises in which someone claims to have figured out the date of Christ's return. In 1843, a minister by the name of William Miller claimed that he cracked the biblical code and predicted that October of 1844 was when Jesus would be coming back. This later became known as 'The Great Disappointment.' Several predictions occurred throughout the 1980s, each obviously not coming to pass. Recently a minister by the name of Harold Camping is predicting that Christ will return May 21, 2011, and has placed billboards all over Memphis, TN with this date of return.

Now I'm all for starting discussions to get society at large talking about Jesus. But the 'more excellent way' is to just follow the blueprint that the Bible outlays. Draw people in with his love, not fear. In Jeremiah 31:3, God says he loves us with an everlasting love, and with lovingkindness has he drawn us. He did not draw us to Him with fear, and he definitely did not draw us in with gimmicks. I call these tactics gimmicks because they are not found in the Bible. If someone is drawn in by fear, they will not stay. If someone comes to God out of fear that the world is going to end on

May 21. On May 22, they are going right back to the club once they realize he's not coming back.

Did not Jesus say he would come back as a thief in the night? He also said that if the owner of the house would have known how the burglar was coming, he would have been prepared for it, and not allowed the break in. If the general population is prepared for when Jesus returns, this passage (Matthew 24) is completely null and void. Nothing against this guy Mr. Camping, but I have to go with Jesus on this one.

The real reason I have a problem with predicting Christ's return is that it's not in line with what He has instructed us to do. Jesus is our Lord, and He has instructed us to complete various specific assignments while we are on the earth.

Let me give an example. Suppose you are wealthy business owner who is about to go away on a leave of absence abroad. While you are away, you give your staff specific assignments to carry out so that the business can run effectively while you are away. For each of your executive staff, you give detailed written instructions on how to complete each task, and even though you are away, you leave your contact number to reach you if any problems arise. Several months go by and you are still not back to your company. A period of a few years go by, and you decide it is time to return. Without warning you return to your office only to find your executive staff has not completed any of the assignments you gave them. Not only that, but the company does not resemble anything like the way you left it and is in debt on the verge of bankruptcy. Your staff still has not seen you return yet, so you anonymously listen to the executive meeting from outside the hallway. In the meeting, they are not discussing objectives or goals, or any of the strategies that you set forth for them to do. Instead, at the meeting they are trying to predict when you are going to return to the office. The company is falling apart because they have not worked in years and the staff is having a heated debate about whether you are going to come back in July of that year, February the following year, or even return at all. How would you respond once you opened that door at the meeting? Would you be pleased with them?

Well God has given us specific assignments to do while He is away. He has instructed us to teach and make disciples of all nations. Preach the Gospel to every creature, lay hands on the sick, deliver the captives, do the same works He did. In fact, He told us to do greater works. 2000 years after He gave these instructions, His company (the church) does not even resemble the way He left it, and most of the employees have not even worked a day after the orientation (getting born again) or even called in for their specific instructions (prayer).

Now let me ask you this question. Do you really want Jesus to come in 2012?

17. The Authority to Heal

Overcoming sickness and disease is much simpler than most "church" people would have you to believe. The reason our ministry has been so successful in overcoming sickness is because we see it for what it really is. Healing the sick is all about a believer understanding their place of authority.

There is *so* much that Jesus did for us 2000 years ago that we are just now beginning to scratch the surface of it. However the point that I want to focus on is this: When Jesus rose from the dead in Matthew 28:18 he said, "All power is given unto me in heaven and in earth." He officially stripped the devil of any power or authority that he had. So Jesus has *all* the power, and we are joint heirs with Him, we are literally in Christ. To be a joint heir means that everything He has, we also have. For example if a wealthy father leaves a joint inheritance for his two sons in the amount of $100 million dollars. That does not mean that each son has $50 million, it means they each jointly have access to that $100 million. In the same way, as we are in Christ, we don't have 'some' power, we have 'ALL' power.

Everything that Jesus could do while He was on the earth, we can do.

The only limitation is in your mind, thinking you are unable or unworthy to have this much power. Yes it takes faith to access this power, but the blood of Jesus has made us right with God, cleansed us of our sins, and therefore we are the rightful joint heirs, sons of the Almighty God.

Is that a lot to digest? Traditionally we have been taught that we are unworthy, that we are nothing but filthy rags; just horrible sinners saved by grace. All that might have been true before we confessed Jesus as Lord, but after the blood has washed us, no longer are we any of these things. We must renew our minds to the divinity of our being, and what exactly the blood has done for us and through us. In Corinthians 5:17, Paul says that if any man be in Christ, he is a new creature, old things are passed away, and everything has become new.

The reality is that you are complete in Christ, full of the Godhead, you just have to be conscious of this and believe it. It will be hard to command sickness to go, or a broken leg to be healed, if in your mind you still feel unworthy, or that you are just a little old worm slithering around. That's why Paul said to let this mind be in you, that was in Christ and to 'put on the mind of Christ'. The truth is that when you go into a situation and speak the Word of God to a demonic spirit that is causing some form of sickness, that demon does not know if it is you speaking or Jesus speaking (and it won't want to risk it being Jesus speaking).

So you have the full authority of Christ, but what are you authorized to do?

Do what Jesus did! 1 John 3:8 says that the sole reason Jesus came was to destroy the works of the devil, so that's what our goal should be too. What are the works of the devil? Sickness, disease, poverty, lack, depression, etc. We have been given authority to destroy all of these works. For a complete list of the works of the devil, or 'the curse' see Deuteronomy 28:15-68. This passage lists what happens when you do not obey God, thus making you susceptible to 'the curse'. Now knowing that you are authorized to destroy the works of the devil, it only makes sense that we exercise this authority by laying hands on the sick, just as Jesus did.

The biggest difference between what we teach and the traditional view of healing in the church, is that the church is looking up to God to do something. Most churches are looking for God to intercede in the lives of people who have sickness, praying that He would heal them. They pray something like, "Lord, please heal brother James, he loves you, we ask you to get involved and heal him in Jesus name. What we do is a little different. God has already done his part. Jesus has already paid the price for every human on the planet to be healed for all eternity. So now that Jesus has done his part, it is on us to take the authority that we have been given and **command** healing. The healing flows through us. Stop looking up to God, to do something he has already given you the authority to do. Our prayers would sound something like this, "In the name of Jesus, I **command** brother James to be healed now. Sickness and disease must go right now, I take authority over any spirit that is illegally operating in His body. Be healed *now*."

Let me give an analogy. Imagine that you are a police officer and you notice an elderly lady across the street from you being robbed by 2 teenagers. Being that you are the police officer on duty, you have your gun, nightstick, tazer, and handcuffs to bring this criminal to justice. So what do you do? You call the police chief down at the headquarters and inform him of the situation and ask if he could come down to where you are and apprehend the criminals. Not only would the chief reprimand you for not handling the situation that you were authorized to handle, but by the time you made the call, the assailants would have robbed the lady and escaped. This sounds crazy right? But this is exactly what the church of today is doing. Instead of dealing with situations they have been authorized to handle, they are trying to get God on the phone to come down and do something.

Just like the police officer, you have been given all the tools you need: the Holy Spirit within you, the Word of God, and angels all around you.

No go make the arrest!!

18. Because of Your Unbelief…

The only time in the Bible that we see Jesus get mad with people is when they had unbelief. In fact, a few times, he would strongly rebuke them, such as in Matt 17:17, in response to their unbelief he says, "You faithless and perverse generation, how much longer am I going to have to put up with you?" I used to read this passage and wonder, why does Jesus have such strong feelings about unbelief. He does not seem express these strong feelings toward his followers about sin, hypocrites, or corruption.

As I began to dig deeper I began to understand that it's not so much that the people did not believe anything. You cannot be held responsible for something you were never exposed to. Non-belief is not believing anything, while unbelief is choosing not to believe. The followers of Jesus literally *refused* to believe the words He spoke. Everything in the Kingdom of God is based upon belief. So without belief, you do not have salvation, healing, deliverance, or anything. 'Unbelief' is one of those spiritual words that through the years does not really have any practical usage in today's society, so let's just call it what it is. If you do not believe the words of Jesus, you are basically calling him a liar. You are basically attributing the chief description of the devil, to Jesus. He is not a liar, there is nothing that He has ever spoken to you or anyone else that has not come to pass, so therefore this is the ultimate insult and form of blasphemy.

Are you calling Him a liar today? Has he given you his word concerning things that He would do for you, and you just brushed His words aside? How would you feel if someone called you a liar? Especially if you never lied, and was not even in your ability to lie? The Word of God is the most powerful thing in this universe, it is the ultimate rock that we can trust and stand on. In John 1, Jesus is defined as the Word which became flesh. Jesus, His Word, and the promises of God are all one. So the next time you just throw away his promises which He declared in his Word, just know that you are calling him a liar.

Why am I making such a big deal about this? It actually is a very serious issue, because according to Jesus in Mark 7, there are only 2 reasons why someone does not receive something we have a right to in the Word of God.

1. Because of their unbelief
2. Their tradition has made the Word of God of no effect.

So over the years, churches have created doctrine and excuses to support their unbelief and unbiblical traditions. Now is the time to remove the veil that has been keeping the masses in darkness for centuries. In the case of healing, when you approach someone, it is based on your faith, not their faith. Many people ask, *'what if they do not believe?'* or *'don't they also have to believe for the healing to work?'* The answer is it really doesn't matter if they believe or not, as long as you believe. It is great if they believe, but don't count on it, as that has nothing to do with what you came to do. Mark 16:18 says, *they shall lay hands on the sick, and they shall recover*; it does not even mention the recipient of the healing. Their job is just to receive. I look at it like I'm going to blast away sickness and disease and anyone that comes in my path is getting healed. It doesn't matter who is in my path!

In the past what many church leaders have done is blame the recipient if they didn't rise up out of a wheelchair, claiming they didn't have enough faith to receive their healing.

If you are praying for the sick, you supply the faith.

Believe His Word, the Word works and cannot fail.

19. Activating the Laws of Healing

Lets imagine for a moment that you and I went back in time to the year 1400. As we were walking down the road, we suddenly see a plane fly over our heads. After being in amazement for a few moments, we say, *'wow, that was a miracle'*. We would say this because something that large is not supposed to be able to fly off the ground, therefore we would say it's a miracle and defies all laws of gravity.

In today's world however, planes are a normal occurrence and we would not call that a miracle. Over the last hundred years, we have discovered the law of lift, which supersedes the law of gravity, and applying this law results in planes, jets, helicopters, and gliders. Ok, Troy, where are you going with this?

When our ministry team is out on the streets or in Wal-Mart or wherever, and we lay hands on someone and they are healed, the crowd looks in amazement and says, *'wow' that is a miracle*. For them, it defies all understanding and is outside of the norm. But for Christian believers this should not be seen as a *'miracle'*, but a normal occurrence for us. Nor is it a one time thing, but a principle and law that has been discovered and is being applied daily. So what law are we using? And can it be applied in any given situation, at any time?

Through the curse of Adam, the whole world became subject to sin, sickness, disease, and lack. Yet through Jesus Christ, we have been made free. So what law are we using? According to Romans 8:2, the law of Spirit of life in Christ Jesus hath made me free from the law of sin and death. Sickness has no legal right to be in my body and when I lay hands on the sick, I minister the life of Christ Jesus and any sickness must go from anyone at anytime.

Now some theologian somewhere will probably try and debate this and say why it will not work and how healing is not for today, much like how the naysayers tried to convince the Wright brothers in 1900 that flying is not possible. John G. Lake, a great man of God who lived about a 100 years ago, demonstrated this scripture as he was ministering in Africa during a time of a great disease outbreak. He wanted to prove to the scientists divine healing, so he applied the frothy diseased particles from a man who recently died and applied it to his arm. Under the microscope they could see the diseased particles literally dying upon contact with his arm. When they asked him how he was able to do this, he explained the law of life in Christ Jesus, and that sickness had no legal right to be on his body.

So what is actually happening here, and how can we apply this law in our lives? In my previous post I explained the supremacy of the kingdom of God. What is actually happening is the kingdom of God is invading Earth and wiping out the effects of the curse. Through Jesus, we have been given authority to bring the kingdom of God to any situation where the curse is involved. In Jesus' prayer, he said, *'Thy kingdom come, thy will be done, on earth as it is in heaven'*. So just as things are in heaven, we have a right to call forth on the earth. If you see a man on crutches, ask yourself if he was in heaven right now, would he be on crutches? No, then call forth the kingdom of heaven right now over his situation on earth, and command him to be healed in Jesus name.

So how do we call the kingdom of God (or heaven) down on the earth exactly? Just how do we activate these laws that you are talking about Troy? Great question, I'm glad you asked.

When Jesus died on the cross and his blood was spilled, the debt was paid for every sickness that has ever existed and will ever happen in the future. It's already been finished, God is not 'going to heal (in the future) anyone, he already took care of it on the cross 2000 years ago. It's so sad when I see people at the altar begging God to heal their Aunt Betty of her disease, saying prayers like, *'Oh won't you please heal her Lord...if you could find it in your heart to heal her...Puleease Lord, heal her.'* I say that this is so sad because he already did everything he is going to do regarding healing, and begging to get God to move is not how it works. It's not that God cannot heal her, and it's not that God is unwilling to heal her, but we have to do our due diligence to find out how to receive the healing that cost Jesus his life 2000 years ago.

So here is how you do it. It's really simple. First of all you must believe. Believe that the work of Jesus is finished, and that everything pertaining to healing is in your hands now. He has given you the power to release it upon the earth. The next step is to activate, or to release the healing by faith. This is done by speaking to whatever is the problem and commanding it be well in Jesus name. Our faith is released when we speak words of authority based upon scripture. For example, if someone has lung cancer, speak directly to the lungs and command the cancer to go. This is what Jesus did, he spoke directly to the fig tree in Mark 11, and then told the disciples to speak directly to a mountain and it would obey them. So speak directly (and don't doubt in your heart) to what the problem is, and then do something you could not do before (if there was stiffness or pain in an area of the body), as this will spark your faith.

So here are some points to remember. It is by grace (a free gift, and gift we didn't deserve) that all mankind is saved, healed, and made whole. Yet we only have access to this grace by faith. It is like a house that is prewired for electricity and lighting. The TV and lights and do not turn on by themselves, you must still flip the switch. Faith is like flipping the switch. We are not working or striving for healing or any of the promises of God, the work has already been done through Christ (just like someone had to go wire the house, set up the lights, and plug in the TV). Just flip the switch!

Believe in the finished work of Christ, activate the healing power of God through faith (speaking it), and watch the power of God transform all of society!

Are you willing to flip the switch?

20. Which Kingdom do You Serve?

The name Jesus literally means deliverer. Its translated name means the same thing as Joshua. And deliverance is exactly what he came to do. For thousands of years, people were enslaved to the demonic kingdom with no way out. Jesus came and made a way out for all of us.

Let's explore this demonic worldly kingdom that the entire world, not freed by Jesus is enslaved to. In Genesis 3:17-19, the curse upon Adam is explained. God says, *'in sorrow and toil shall you eat [of the fruits] all the days of your life. Thorns and thistles shall it bring forth for you, and you shall eat the plants of the field. In the sweat of your face shall you eat bread until you return to the ground.'* The modern translation of this would sound like this: You will work like a dog for six days a week to feed your family. From the time you are of age until you are old you will work for a living, live in debt to pay for your house, your car and that you will not even own, and be miserable doing so, at a job you can't stand.

Is this really so? In the United States, less than 2% of people actually own their own homes (paid in full). People are drowning in debt, underpaid with little hope of relief. Why does everyone 'want to be a millionaire'? Why is there is such an appeal to the lottery? It's not so people can drive around in fancy cars and big mansions, it's because people believe that if they had a million dollars they would have relief. They would not have to go to work in the morning. They would not have to work so hard just pay off mounting debts.

But the bottom line is that this is exactly what Jesus came to do. Give you freedom from that worldly system, that demonic kingdom. According 1 John 3:8, Jesus came to the earth to destroy the works of the devil. The effects of the curse was this slavery to overwhelming debt, sickness, poverty, and more. But the million dollar question is this, what did Jesus actually do? What did he actually teach? The average Christian will tell you that Jesus came to die for our sins. This is in fact true, but this is just scratching the surface of his teaching.

Jesus came to introduce a new system. A new way of life, the kingdom of God. In fact, this was his message wherever he preached. He described how amazing the kingdom of God was in various descriptive parables.

The message that Jesus preached, the kingdom of God, was the supremacy of God's way over everything on the earth. Supremacy over sickness, supremacy over lack, everything. The constitution of the kingdom of God is the Word of God. There is nothing pertaining to mankind that is not addressed by the Word of God. He introduced a way in which mankind would have an escape from all of the toils the world was suffering, complaining, and slaving about.

Now at this point, everything that I have said, most Christians agree with. They know the Word of God is infallible. They know it is supreme. But knowing about it is not enough. You must believe it, activate it, live it, and be able to demonstrate the fruits of it in your life. Jesus did not just *'talk'* about the kingdom of God, he demonstrated its power everywhere he went.

A friend of mine who was recently diagnosed with a disease, asked me if I could give her some extra insight into healing. As if I knew something *'extra'* about the Word that she did not. I told her I know the same scriptures concerning healing as you do. I told her, its real simple, either you believe them and act in faith, or you don't.

See, most Christians verbally agree with the kingdom of God, but they actually live in the world's demonic system. They claim Jesus is their healer, yet go to the doctors before consulting Him. If they need money they use credit cards or a bank for a loan. If they have a question about an important decision, some even consult a psychic. It's a direct slap in the face to God.

Matthew 6:19-34 highlights the difference between the two systems, and also gives us 2 easy ways in which we can know which system we are actually living under. Jesus says, 'Seek ye first the kingdom of God and his righteousness, and all these things shall be added to you.' What things is he talking about? All the things the people without God are striving to get: shelter, food, cars, jobs, etc. So how do you know which system you are under? The first way we can know is: Which kingdom/system do you go to first when there is a problem?

If there is a pain in your chest whose kingdom do you run to? Do you go to the hospital, and get an opinion from the doctor? Then get a second opinion, 3rd opinion and 4th

opinion. And then when all else fails you cry out to God on your deathbed months later? If a bill comes out of nowhere what do you do? Do you get a 2nd and 3rd job, take out a loan from the bank, max out your credit cards, and then decide to consult the Lord if you should 'give an offering, so you can receive.'
The other way you find out which system/kingdom you are serving is found in Matt 6:21, where you treasure is, there your heart will be also. Who are you financially supporting?

The kingdom of God is not some great mystery in which we cannot live there daily. It far surpasses the world's way in every possible way. Divine health, happy marriage, more than enough money for you to live, and peace of mind, are all aspects of God's kingdom; but you must make it up in your mind that that is where you are going to live and totally divorce yourself from the world's way, no matter how appealing it seems. The devil is a master of deception, so his way will appear to be more attractive (just ask Eve), but it always ends the same: hurt, sadness, lack, and defeat.

In my previous teachings we have discussed demonstrating the kingdom of God, and how to enter in the kingdom, how to activate the benefits of the kingdom, but 1st you must determine in your mind that you will never go back to the world's inferior system. Jesus made it really simple when he said a man cannot serve 2 masters, so pick which one you will serve.

Christian people have mastered the art of religion, and being fake. According to Hebrews 11, it is impossible to please God without faith. It's not like you can honestly think you can say to God, *'I love you with all my heart, I just don't believe anything you say'* and think He would be pleased with you. In church services all across the US, people have a form of godliness: praising God, and acting as if they are people of faith, but let's look at your calendar and your checkbook and then we can really see if you have faith

21. Prosperity Gone Wrong

I literally cringe every time I hear someone twist up the Gospel. The core message is simple and direct, even though it is not being preached in 98% of churches across the country. When the foundation is off, everything else will be off as well.

I recently heard someone say to me, '*God does everything I ask Him to do*' and '*Everything I do is a success*'. Now these may seem trivial and harmless on the surface, but if we examine a little deeper we expose the root of this way of thinking. Is there really a problem with making our own plans and agendas and getting God to bless it? The million dollar question is this: Whose vision are you really following?

Let's take a step back. If we examine Christian history over the past 100 years or so, we can see how God has moved and where He is moving today. During this time, many things were revealed to the body of Christ including the baptism of the Holy Spirit (tongues), the healing gifts, miracles, and activation of the prophetic gifts just to name a few. During the last 30 years or so, a revelation of the seed was introduced, and how God will prosper you financially. The Holy Spirit has revealed this to the body of Christ, and I'm not here to debate whether or not God wants you healed, or whether or not he wants you doing well financially. The core issue at hand is *what is your motive? What is your intention?* Over the past few years many have perverted the message of financially prosperity, and I cringe whenever I perceive it.

Yes, God will bless you financially. Yes, He promised in His Word that you would be whole, but many miss out what it is all based on. Jesus must be Lord of your life. When you come to the Lord, you forsake all and follow Him. You were bought with a price (the blood), so your life no longer exists, you live the life of Jesus from now on. So many people get hurt in churches that teach about financially prosperity because they neglect this truth. In fact, Jesus is not Lord over their life. Tthey are masquerading as Christians when in fact they have their own agenda and use the name of Jesus for their own selfish gain. Jesus said, 'My sheep hear **my voice**.' He also said, 'Why call me Lord Lord and do not the things I say'.

Kobe Bryant gets his salary from the Lakers, by playing for the Lakers. Bill Gates gets his income from Microsoft, by doing the work he does for Microsoft. But why do we have Christians, who do not work for the kingdom of God, and expect God to bless them? We have many who call themselves Christians, but how many are actually disciples of Jesus? How many actually have Him as their Lord?

I'm not against anyone having material things like nice cars or houses, but according to Matthew 6, the blueprint for receiving those things in the kingdom of God is to seek Him *first*, and they will be added to you. Because most Christians operate in the world system through debt, instead of them having nice things, those nice things have them. In fact they are enslaved to them.

The raw truth of the matter is that the concept of 'me first' and 'I'll make my plans and get God to bless them' is not Biblically based at all. It is a perversion of Christianity that is actually secular humanism. In secular humanism, the center of everything is you. Your happiness and well being is above everything else. God exists to please me and meet my every demand. It's not about what heaven wants to do, it's about what you want to do. This is totally against everything that Jesus taught. Verbally, secular humanists will confess to love God and be Christians, but everything in their lives lines up with the world system instead of the Word of God.

The message that is not being preached is that when you come to Christ, you surrender all and He becomes your Lord. You are dead, and your new life is hid in Christ. Stop trying resurrect that dead person. Jesus is now your source and responsible for you, **but only *if you let him***. I ask you a question today, is he your source? When you have a financial hardship, is He your source? or is the bank your source, begging them for a loan. When sickness comes, do you go to the Word, and seek Him as the source for your healing? Or do you run straight to the doctors and prescription pills.

In God's system, we go to him first to see what His plans are. Then we must line up with the visions and promptings of the Holy Spirit to accomplish these plans. A vision, according to Proverbs 29:18 AMP, is a redemptive revelation of God. So any plan, business, or motive, that is not a redemptive revelation of God, would not qualify as a vision. Lastly, make this vision the most important thing in your life, it is why you were created. In Rick Warren's the Purpose Driven life, the first line of the book states, it's not about you. I agree 100%. This is not a selfish thing, the vision is all about other people. In return, God blesses you as you are a blessing to others.

One of the most presumptuous things you can say is 'God is on *my* side'. That is both unwise and unscriptural. In Joshua 5:13, Joshua saw a spiritual being with his outstretched sword, and asked him, *'Are you for us, or our adversaries.'* The being responded, *'Neither, I am the Prince of the Lord's Army.'* Yet Joshua was wise enough to join *that* side. Today, we would be wise to join God's side, and not assume he's on *our* side. If you are not on God's side, you are on the enemy's side by default.

God's way is better in every way. His system will keep you healthier over your lifetime, and will provide financial stability for you regardless of the economy. Leave the collapsing world system and follow God's system wholeheartedly. Stop trying to have one foot in both worlds, it does not work that way, a man cannot serve two masters. It's like Kobe Bryant having a multimillion dollar contract with the Lakers, but deciding instead to make his living playing pickup basketball on the streets for money.

Choose you this day who you will serve.

Conclusion

Hopefully after reading these teachings you have been inspired to go out and do something. It was not intended for you to just read it and say, *'that was very interesting'*. The whole intent was to get you to do the same thing we are out here doing. There is no special anointing that I have or any other Christian has that makes him/her able to do what you cannot. In Christ we are all equal. We all have access to the same Holy Spirit, which empowers us. We are to do the same workings that Jesus did, even greater because his ministry on earth was only for 3 and a half years. I heard one preacher say one time that if this glorious gospel does not cause you to move…then it has not moved you yet!

This is not just a book, it's a movement...

Get Involved today!

How to Stay Connected With Us:

www.demonstrateit.org

twitter @troyanthonysmit

facebook.com/demonstrateit

www.ingramcontent.com/pod-product-compliance
Lightning Source LLC
Chambersburg PA
CBHW061449040426
42450CB00007B/1286